ANIMAL RELATIVES

CATS and LIONS

FELINE RELATIVES

by Dionna L. Mann

PEBBLE
a capstone imprint

Published by Pebble, an imprint of Capstone
1710 Roe Crest Drive, North Mankato, Minnesota 56003
capstonepub.com

Copyright © 2026 by Capstone. All rights reserved. No part of this publication may be reproduced in whole or in part, or stored in a retrieval system, or transmitted in any form or by any means, electronic, mechanical, photocopying, recording, or otherwise, without written permission of the publisher.

Library of Congress Cataloging-in-Publication Data
is available on the Library of Congress website.
ISBN: 9798875220241 (hardcover)
ISBN: 9798875220197 (paperback)
ISBN: 9798875220203 (ebook PDF)

Summary: Did you know that house cats and lions are actually related? They have similar physical features and behaviors, including grooming, climbing, and using their whiskers to sense what's around them. But lions are huge and roam grasslands with other lions. Cats live with people or in groups outdoors. Explore the many amazing ways cats and lions are alike and different. Learn about the habitats, skills, life cycles, and features of these feline relatives.

Editorial Credits
Editor: Ashley Kuehl; Designer: Bobbie Nuytten; Media Researcher: Svetlana Zhurkin; Production Specialist: Whitney Schaefer

Image Credits
Capstone: Bobbie Nuytten, 21 (bottom); Getty Images: 500x/Fredrik Findahl, 21 (top), George Pachantouris, 15, krblokhin, 28, Martin Harvey, 27, McDonald Wildlife Photography Inc., 23, Michael J. Cohen, 10, Rixipix, 5; Shutterstock: Anna Zaro, 12, Astrid Gast, 4, bdavid32, 9 (bottom), Carl Lorenz Overleashing, 8, Daniel Danckwerts, 13, Irina Kozorog, 9 (top), Liubomyr Tryhubyshyn, cover (top), Markovka (background), cover, 1, 30, Maurizio Bersanelli, 29, mdsharifPG, 20, meunierd, cover (bottom), Robby Holmwood, 25, Sandor Gora, 24, Seregraff, 6, Seyms Brugger, 7, Spirit9, 19, Thomas Curry, 16, vlalukinv, 14, yhelfman, 17, Zelma Brezinska, 11

Any additional websites and resources referenced in this book are not maintained, authorized, or sponsored by Capstone. All product and company names are trademarks™ or registered® trademarks of their respective holders.

TABLE OF CONTENTS

Cat Cousins 4

Body Check 6

A Mother's Care 8

Fierce Hunters 10

The Way They Move 14

Body Talk 16

Measuring Up 20

Feline Families 22

Watch Out! 26

Snooze Fest 28

    Can You Remember? 30

    Animal Jokes 30

    Glossary 31

    Index 32

    About the Author 32

Words in **bold** are in the glossary.

CAT COUSINS

Is it true? A cute little kitty is **kin** to a roaring lion? It's true, all right! Cats and lions are whiskered cousins.

Cats and lions are alike in many ways. But they have differences too. Let's take a look.

FUN FACT

Cats and lions are called felines. Both are in the animal family *Felidae*.

BODY CHECK

The bodies of cats and lions are the same in many ways. Their legs move in the same way. Their mouths are full of sharp, strong teeth. Both have fur coats. They both have tails that flick. They have ears that turn.

Male and female cats look alike. Lions look different. A male lion wears a big, furry mane. A female does not.

A MOTHER'S CARE

Cats and lions give birth to live young. A baby cat is a kitten. A baby lion is a cub. Kittens and cubs **nurse** for many weeks after birth. They drink their mother's milk.

Mother cats and lions carry babies in their mouths. They grab the loose skin on the baby's neck.

Cat and lion mothers **groom** their young by licking them. Cat and lion tongues have tiny, hard **spines**. They clean and smooth fur.

FIERCE HUNTERS

Cats and lions are meat-eating hunters. Lions often hunt at dusk and dawn. The sun is sinking or beginning to rise. Outdoor cats hunt at this time of day too.

Cats and lions can see in low light. They have amazing night vision. Their ears can hear the smallest sounds. That helps them find **prey** in the dark.

Cats and lions both have whiskers. These help them feel their way around. The hunters can find their prey.

Lions and cats have pads on their paws. The pads let them walk quietly. They can sneak up on their prey and . . . pounce! Time for lunch!

a lion's paw

Cat and lion paws have a toe that sticks out. It is a dewclaw. The dewclaw helps them hold their prey.

13

THE WAY THEY MOVE

Cats use their claws to climb. They may climb cat trees or shelves. Cats like to watch the world from above.

Some lions climb trees. They watch what's going on. But most lions prefer to be on the ground.

Cats and lions have strong hind legs. Both animals can run, leap, jump, and twirl. If they fall, they can twist and turn. That helps them land on their feet.

BODY TALK

Cats and lions talk with their bodies. They yawn if they are sleepy. Cubs and kittens tumble and paw when they want to play.

Scared cats run away. Even a mighty lion will take cover when facing danger.

Enemies, watch out! Cats and lions may show their teeth and pull out their claws. Their tails twitch back and forth.

Lions roar to tell others to back off. When lions roar together, they send a message. They tell other lions that this is their land. They say, hunt somewhere else.

Cats do not roar. They hiss as a warning to others. But when cats feel content, they purr. Lions do not purr. They grunt, gurgle, or moan when they feel good.

FUN FACT

A lion's roar can be heard up to 5 miles (8 kilometers) away!

MEASURING UP

Female lions can weigh up to 350 pounds (159 kilograms). They can be almost 6 feet (2 meters) long. That's without their tails! Adult males can weigh up to 500 pounds (227 kg). They can grow up to 8 feet (2.4 m) long!

House cats are much smaller. Most house cats weigh 8 to 15 pounds (3.6 to 6.8 kg). Their head and body are about 18 inches (46 centimeters) long.

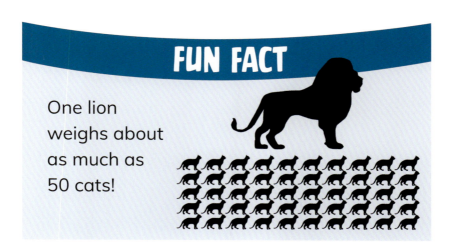

FUN FACT

One lion weighs about as much as 50 cats!

FELINE FAMILIES

A group of lions is called a pride. It is a close family. A pride can have several females. It often has a few males too. In each pride, a strong male protects everyone. All the lions look after the cubs.

A pride can have as few as four lions. Or it can have up to 30 lions! The **average** is 15.

Wild outdoor cats form **colonies**. Females stick together. They look after one another's kittens.

In a human home, kittens often form close bonds with their humans. Sometimes they make friends with a family dog.

Lions and cats both rub their heads on family members. This puts their **scent** on them. The animals are showing that they belong together.

WATCH OUT!

Wild lions might look cuddly, but watch out! One swipe of a paw can be deadly! Most lions are **wary** of humans. Humans are wary of lions too.

Cats that live outdoors without humans are feral cats. Feral cats are wary of humans.

Some humans have raised lion cubs as they would kittens. These cubs bond with the humans. But wildlife experts agree that this is a bad idea.

SNOOZE FEST

Cats and lions spend many hours sleeping. Outdoor cats like to sleep in the shade. Cats inside might snooze in a warm, sunny spot.

Both cats and lions sleep in many positions. They might curl in a ball, lie flat, or lie on their side. They might even sleep on their backs with paws in the air.

Next time you see a cat or a lion, see what you notice! What is alike and different?

CAN YOU REMEMBER?

1. What body part do cats and lions use to groom their babies?

2. What three sense organs help cats and lions make their way in the dark?

3. What part of cat and lion paws allows them to sneak up on their prey?

4. What is the name of a family of lions that roams together?
   - a.) colony
   - b.) pride
   - c.) pod

5. True or False: A feral cat will make a good pet.

Check your answers at the bottom of page 31!

ANIMAL JOKES

What do you call a cat who makes no errors on a test?
A purr-fect scorer.

Why did the zebra run when the lion said she wanted to be friends?
The zebra was sure she was lyin'.

Why did the lion cross the road?
To get to the other pride.

Why did the cat join the band?
She wanted to make mew-sic.

GLOSSARY

average (AV-ur-ij)—the way most things are

colony (KAH-luh-nee)—a group of animals that live together

groom (GROOM)—to clean the coat of an animal by washing, scrubbing, and brushing

kin (KIN)—related animals or people

nurse (NURS)—to feed a baby milk from its mother

prey (PRAY)—an animal that is hunted to be eaten by another animal

scent (SENT)—a smell made by an animal that acts as a signal to other animals

spines (SPYNZ)—sharp spikes that grow on a plant or animal

wary (WAIR-ee)—careful or aware of danger

1. tongue, 2. eyes (sight), ears (hearing), and whiskers (touch), 3. pads, 4. b.) pride, 5. False

INDEX

claws, 14, 17
climbing, 14
colonies, 24
communication, 16–18
cubs, 8, 16, 22, 26
dewclaws, 13
felines, 5
fur, 6–7, 9

grooming, 9
hearing, 6, 11
humans, 24, 26
hunting, 10–13, 18
kittens, 8, 16, 24, 26
paws, 12–13, 26, 29
prides, 22

scent, 25
size, 20–21
sleeping, 28–29
sounds, 11, 18
tails, 6, 17, 20
teeth, 6, 17
vision, 11
whiskers, 4, 12

ABOUT THE AUTHOR

Dionna L. Mann is a children's book author who spent nearly 25 years working and volunteering in her local school system. As an independent researcher, she especially enjoys discovering lesser-known individuals shining in the margins of African American history. Dionna's debut novel for young readers, *Mama's Chicken & Dumplings* (Margaret Ferguson Books, 2024) was chosen as a Junior Library Guild Gold Selection. Find Dionna online at dionnalmann.com.